Who Was
Wilma Mankiller?

by Andrea Page

illustrated by Stephen Marchesi

Penguin Workshop

To Wilma and the powerful women—
past to present—who inspire me
to meet life's challenges with courage,
determination, and resilience—AP

PENGUIN WORKSHOP
An imprint of Penguin Random House LLC
1745 Broadway, New York, New York 10019

First published in the United States of America by Penguin Workshop,
an imprint of Penguin Random House LLC, 2025

Visit us online at penguinrandomhouse.com.

Library of Congress Cataloging-in-Publication Data is available.

Printed in the United States of America

ISBN 9780593888872 (paperback)   10 9 8 7 6 5 4 3 2 1 CJKW
ISBN 9780593888889 (library binding)   10 9 8 7 6 5 4 3 2 1 CJKW

The authorized representative in the EU for product safety and compliance
is Penguin Random House Ireland, Morrison Chambers, 32 Nassau Street,
Dublin D02 YH68, Ireland, https://eu-contact.penguin.ie.

Contents

Who Was Wilma Mankiller?

Wilma P. Mankiller was not a follower but a leader.

In 1956, the United States convinced Wilma's father, Charley Mankiller, that moving to a big city would offer him and his family more opportunities. When Wilma was ten years old, she didn't want to follow her father's decision to move to San Francisco. Leaving the Cherokee reservation in Oklahoma meant losing everything, including their community. But she respected her parents and tried to adapt to her new environment.

Wilma didn't belong in San Francisco. She was a country girl, not a city girl. She held on to her Cherokee identity even as she tried to fit in. Reflecting on the courage of her relatives who came before her gave her strength. Wilma knew that in 1838, the US government had forced the Cherokee people, along with several other Native American tribes, to leave their ancestral homelands and start their lives over in a different place. This forced relocation was called the Trail of Tears.

Wilma compared her life in San Francisco to her ancestors' lives. Even though they lost everything, they still survived. Their resiliency gave her courage to do the same. With "a good mind" (a Cherokee value), Wilma believed in herself and tackled her problems.

After two decades in California, Wilma led her daughters, Felicia and Gina, back to Oklahoma. She wanted her children to develop a strong connection to their Cherokee heritage, land, and community.

However, things had changed during Wilma's long absence. Her childhood home on Mankiller Flats had burned down years before. Only traces of their vegetable garden and the spring they drank from remained.

"When we first moved back," Wilma recalled, "I felt as though folks welcomed us, but for a while, they seemed to treat us more like company than family." She remembered having a stronger connection to her community. But she followed a new path with her compassion and strong work ethic. By using her skills to write grants to fund projects, she helped the neediest communities improve their homes and schools. By reaching out to help others, she warmed people's hearts.

During this time, Wilma met Principal Chief Ross O. Swimmer, the highest-ranking leader in the Cherokee Nation. He noticed her determination. Rural Cherokee communities faced hardships, and he saw how Wilma humbly worked alongside community members.

Principal Chief Ross O. Swimmer

During her career as a public servant, Wilma struggled with many physical illnesses. But she felt all her experiences were important. As she said later in life, "I realized I could survive anything.

I had faced adversity and turned it into a positive experience—a better path."

Although she faced many obstacles, Wilma relied on her abilities and maintained a positive outlook on life.

When Wilma had first moved back to Oklahoma, little did she know she would go on to make history as the first woman to lead the Cherokee Nation. As the next principal chief after Ross O. Swimmer, Wilma P. Mankiller brought her community together. The way she lived her life is a source of inspiration for many and will be for generations to come.

CHAPTER 1
Growing Up on Mankiller Flats

Wilma Pearl Mankiller was born on November 18, 1945, at W. W. Hastings Indian Hospital in Tahlequah, Oklahoma. Her parents, Charley Mankiller and Clara Sitton Mankiller, had eleven children together. Wilma was their sixth.

Charley came from a long line of Cherokee Mankillers in an area called Indian Country in Oklahoma. Clara's ancestors were Dutch and Irish. When Wilma was young, she was called by her middle name, Pearl, after her maternal grandmother.

Wilma and her siblings grew up with other families in their Cherokee community. People living there are familiar with family names like Hummingbird, Wolf, Beaver, Soap, Canoe, Walkingstick, Gourd, and many others. Those were common surnames in Adair County, where the family lived.

Mankiller was a name of honor with a unique importance in her tribe. Wilma discovered that important leaders from the past held the title of Mankiller, which was a respected military rank. "I am proud . . . [and] hope to honor my ancestors by keeping the name alive," Wilma later said.

The Mankiller family moved into their home in 1948 after Charley and his uncle, Looney Gourd, built the house on Mankiller Flats. Rough lumber made up the framework of the four-room home. A tin roof protected them from the weather.

The house had sparse furniture and a woodstove for cooking. Wilma and her siblings had to haul water for drinking and washing from a nearby spring. The spring also served as a refrigerator, keeping bottles of milk cool. When Wilma needed light, she used a coal-oil lamp. When Wilma needed a bathroom, she used an outdoor toilet called an outhouse. Sometimes at Christmas, Wilma received marbles or jacks and some fruit or candy as gifts. Like many families in the rural Rocky Mountain community,

An outhouse

the Mankillers were considered "dirt poor." According to Wilma's recollection, "We were on the bottom rung of the poverty ladder."

Families grew large vegetable gardens and harvested foods from nature. Wilma's mother knew the names of every edible plant, bush, or flower in the woods near their home.

They gathered dandelion greens and various types of berries. They dug wild onions and vegetables from their garden. They fished for catfish, caught frogs, and hunted. Various types of bird meat filled their plates. They also ate a lot of squirrel. Wilma's mother used breadcrumbs to coat the small pieces of meat, then she would fry them and make gravy from the drippings. Or she'd make squirrel soup with dumplings. Wilma thought squirrel tasted a little like chicken. She was glad her family never went hungry.

According to Wilma, from the day her mother married her father, her mother's life "became centered around Cherokee family life," and Wilma learned to speak both Cherokee and English at home. She relied on a community of aunts, uncles, and neighbors. And when everyone came together for ceremonial dances, the adults danced all night, so the kids had no bedtime. They played hide-and-seek and other games together as long as they wanted.

Visiting relatives and listening to stories provided entertainment. Wilma loved her father's stories, even the scary ones. "One time, Dad told us, someone in our area shot an owl with a silver bullet. The next day, mysteriously, the person learned that his most bitter enemy had been found shot to death." Some Native people consider owls to be messengers of death.

The Mankiller family drove on weekend trips to Stilwell, Oklahoma, in an old black 1949

Ford. Stilwell was much bigger than the Rocky Mountain community where they lived. For Wilma, visiting with her Uncle Tom and Aunt Maud Sitton and attending the annual strawberry festival in May were highlights. It was exciting because the kids got to spend a dime on either a movie or a bag of candy.

Prizewinning strawberries

Wilma remembered visiting other relatives, too, including her great-aunt (also named Wilma

Mankiller), who gave them clothes and other gifts. Her father's half sister, Jensie Hummingbird, had jet-black hair, made her own cotton dresses, and spoke only Cherokee. Aunt Maude Wolfe, her father's cousin, loved working outside and playing traditional Cherokee stickball. She helped keep the community's ceremonial grounds looking nice.

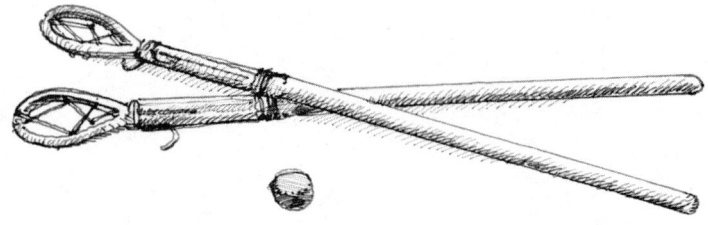

Cherokee stickball sticks and game ball

Her husband, Uncle Jim Wolfe, knew traditional medicines, led ceremonial dances, and had a witty sense of humor. Wilma was most content when surrounded by her relatives.

Great-aunt Maggie Gourd left a big impression on Wilma. She and her brother Johnny loved listening to Aunt Maggie's adventure stories about the old days, which sometimes involved gunmen, bank robbers, and hidden treasures. Afterward, they'd trade eggs with her for fresh milk and be on their way.

Wilma's favorite pastime was playing in the woods. Sometimes she'd sneak away instead of doing her chores. Being in nature was like being in an outdoor classroom. Wilma also liked to read. She gained a love of literature from her father. "A love for books and reading was one of the best gifts he ever gave his children," she wrote.

One of Wilma's earliest memories was sitting on a trunk (a large chest used as luggage) after her family moved into their "little bitty house full of too many people." Wilma felt happy and whole spending time with her family at Mankiller Flats. But soon, everything she knew about her life would change.

CHAPTER 2
History Repeats Itself

Young Wilma was often shy. She hid in the attic when non-Native people came to Mankiller Flats. One day, she heard her mother and father speaking with a stranger, a white man who worked as a United States government agent for the Bureau of Indian Affairs (BIA). He told Wilma's parents that relocating, or moving, to a big city would be a wonderful opportunity. But the BIA agent's promise hid a goal of assimilation—the process of adopting the customs and culture of another group. The United States government wanted Native people to become part of more mainstream American society. Government actions targeted Native people, customs, and traditions that had been in place for decades.

From the late 1800s to the mid-1900s, the US government broke earlier treaty agreements, reduced reservation lands, and ended the tribal status of many nations to erase Indigenous culture. BIA agents offered relocation to families to weaken tribal nations and gain more land.

Now it was 1956, and the ongoing conversation scared Wilma. She feared her parents would move their family to a new place, which meant she'd have to leave her community. Wilma loved her extended Cherokee family, and she didn't want to leave them.

Her father, Charley, and her mother, Clara, considered what the government agent promised: a better-paying job and a home with indoor plumbing, electricity, telephones, and other things they did not have. The agent convinced Wilma's dad to move his family across the country and leave poverty behind. Wilma didn't like the idea of moving away.

Assimilation, Termination, and Relocation

In 1953, the United States government established a federal policy of termination, ending its responsibilities to more than sixty tribal nations. The government removed their tribal identities and stole their land in an attempt to dissolve Indian reservations.

In 1956, the Indian Relocation Act (Public Law 959) broke up even more Native nations. The government created a program to move Native families to a city of their choice. Then, it promised to help them with housing and jobs in several cities, including Chicago, Denver, Los Angeles, San Francisco, San Jose, St. Louis, Cincinnati, Cleveland, and Dallas. The agents used promotional brochures showing relocated families in new homes with smiles on their faces. These advertisements convinced people that life would be better in a big city.

By terminating tribal identities and relocating families, the US government could then sell the reservation land.

An advertisement for the
American Indian Urban Relocation Program

In October 1956, her parents sold everything, including the family car. One month before Wilma's eleventh birthday, they gathered their possessions and rode in a neighbor's car to a train station in Stilwell, Oklahoma. Wilma later wrote that at the time, "Dad was also worried, but he was excited about the chance for a better life for all of us."

As they huddled together, Wilma felt lost. She couldn't imagine what California was like.

As the car pulled onto the gravel road, she watched as their homeland, where her family had lived for generations, passed by. Wilma noticed her home become smaller in the distance, then disappear behind them. They passed the store and her school. She tried to remember every detail. As they drove  past the woodlands, Wilma tried to memorize the shape of every tree. She filled her mind with familiar sounds: the cheerful singing of birds, coyotes howling in the distance, crickets chirping at night. Mankiller Flats was her home. She belonged in Oklahoma.

Wilma had never been very far from her home. Her entire world was in Oklahoma. Other than a school field trip to a nearby town, she stayed close to her farm. It's where she felt safe. She called the move her own "little Trail of Tears."

Once the family arrived in Stilwell, they stopped at a restaurant for their last taste of Oklahoma—a chili dinner—before walking to the train station.

All the children experienced riding a train for the first time. Wilma heard a whistle and a loud whoosh as they chugged north away from the station. She felt the rocking motion in her seat and watched the countryside go by in a blur outside her window. "As soon as we were all on the train, my sister Frances started to cry," Wilma later wrote. "It seemed as if she cried without stopping all the way from Oklahoma to California."

The Trail of Tears

The Cherokee people had lived in what are now parts of Georgia, Alabama, Tennessee, Kentucky, West Virginia, Virginia, North Carolina, and South Carolina for thousands of years.

In the early 1800s, the Cherokee Nation resisted pressure from the US government to give up their land and move west of the Mississippi River. Then the Indian Removal Act of 1830 forced all southeastern tribes to leave their ancestral homelands.

The removal took several years. From 1830 to 1839, about five thousand US Army troops removed not only Cherokee people but also people from other tribes, including the Choctaw, Chickasaw, Creek, and Seminole. People from the five tribes walked thousands of miles in all kinds of weather. Disease spread through the camps. Many people grew sick and died. One-quarter of the Cherokee population perished on what came to be known as the Trail of Tears.

The paths of the Trail of Tears

Those who survived worked hard to reestablish their Cherokee Nation near present-day Tahlequah, Oklahoma. The survivors were determined to preserve their language, education, and government.

Wilma and her family rode the train for two days and two nights. They passed through Riverbank, California, where Clara's mother, Grandmother Sitton, lived. The train chugged on for another ninety miles, at last stopping at their destination, San Francisco. Soon, they found out that the US government had not kept its promises.

To Wilma, everything seemed hopeless in San Francisco because she had nowhere to run and hide in her new city environment.

CHAPTER 3
A Different Life in San Francisco

Everything the government agent assured the Mankillers about moving to San Francisco had been a lie. Instead of having a nice place to live, a shabby hotel room was the only option. There were no apartments available when they arrived. The Relocation Act agreed to pay hotel costs for four weeks but only paid for two. Then the Mankillers had to find their own apartment. The BIA agents who had been hired to assist families in finding higher-paying jobs didn't help Charley find one. What was promised did not come true.

Wilma's father and her oldest brother, Don, found jobs at a rope factory. Making ropes wasn't what Wilma's father had planned. Every day both men walked to work and the kids went to school.

It wasn't better than before. For Wilma, it was even worse.

Her name caught people's attention in her fifth-grade classroom. "When the teacher came to my name during roll call each morning," Wilma recalled, "every single person laughed."

That was new to Wilma.

"The other kids also teased me about the way I talked and dressed," Wilma later wrote. Growing up in the country with long black hair and homemade clothes was all she knew. She felt out of place with her classmates, like a weed sticking out on a city sidewalk. "I was never truly comfortable in the schools of California." She had lost the safety of her old life in Oklahoma. But just like a dandelion, she grew strength from her roots.

Wilma and her sister attempted to make things better. After completing their dinner and homework, the girls spent their evenings reading to each other, trying to speak like their classmates who didn't have Oklahoma accents. They talked about their memories of home on Mankiller Flats. Their strong connection helped the girls feel most at peace. This strategy helped them survive tough times. "I continue to think about the past and to circle back to my tribal history for doses of comfort," Wilma said later in life.

During their free time in the first weeks in California, Wilma and her siblings explored their hotel. She recalled, "No one had bothered to even try to prepare us for city living." Everything was new and different. She spent her days surrounded by crowds, traffic, and skyscrapers. "We might as well have been on the far side of the moon."

One day, Wilma and her brother Richard were walking the halls in the hotel when suddenly a wall opened up. People entered, and the doors closed as they watched. After a short while, the doors opened and a new group of people appeared. Since they had never seen an elevator before, they took the stairs instead. Life here was unlike anything Wilma had experienced before.

In Oklahoma, Wilma could find peace and quiet by running outdoors. "My dad always described me as a sunny child," Wilma mentioned in an interview later in life. But in San Francisco, neon lights flickered through the night. Loud honking and ambulance sirens filled the air. She felt helpless, like a rabbit surrounded by wolves. Wilma's sunny attitude faded.

She hated school. She hated the city. Remembering her Cherokee history helped ease her fear. She found comfort in remembering the resilience of her people. Her ancestors lost everything, walked for days to settle in a new place, and survived. She would, too.

Her father and brother saved enough money in a year to buy a house in a new neighborhood. They moved out of their cramped hotel room and settled into a small house in the town of Daly City. But things didn't change much for Wilma. She was still a country girl surrounded by an unfriendly city.

In Daly City, Wilma started seventh grade and felt more alone than ever. She couldn't talk to her parents about her situation of not fitting in. They were too busy. Her father worked tirelessly to put food on the table and keep a roof over their heads. Her mom took care of their eleven children, as well as the cooking and cleaning.

But the Mankillers were not alone in that situation. San Francisco became a new home for thousands of Native American families who left poor rural towns for poor urban settings.

Eventually, they found one another. Native American community centers formed. They met people from other tribes. Dinners, meetings, sewing clubs, and dances brought the intertribal community closer.

Wilma and her sister spent time at the American Indian Center babysitting. On Saturday nights, Wilma and Linda watched women put on makeup and style their hair. The smell of Aqua Net hairspray filled the room as ladies styled their hair into beehive hairdos, a popular trend at that time.

Native American or American Indian?

How do you know when to use the term *Native American* or *American Indian*?

Most historical documents use the term *American Indian*. But as language develops, some terms change. Currently, *Native American* is a term used to describe Native people living in the United States, including Alaska and Hawaii.

First Nations is commonly used to describe Native people living in Canada. *Aboriginal* people are the first inhabitants in Australia. And *Indigenous* is a term used to describe Native nations around the world. All of the terms are used today; however, many Native people prefer to be called by their specific tribal name.

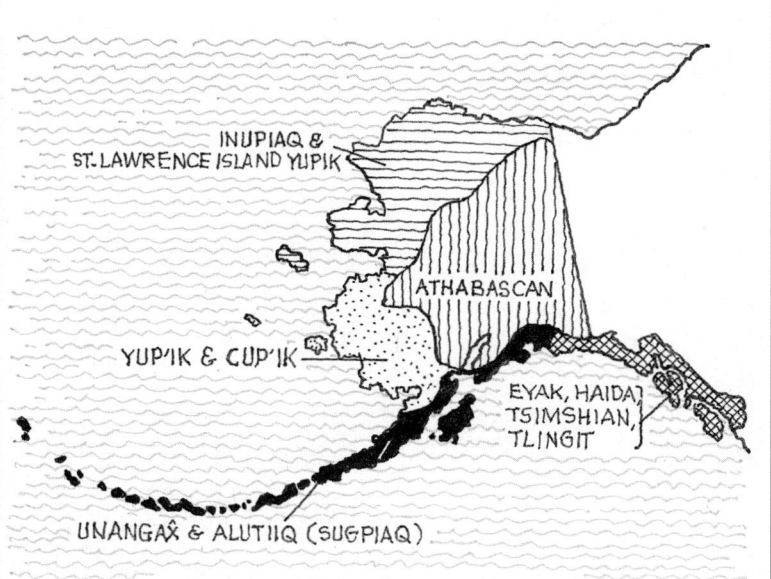

Territories of Alaska Native cultures

Wilma had a plan and set aside her babysitting money. When she saved enough, she bought a bus ticket to Riverbank, California, which was about ninety miles away. She ran away, she thought, to a safer place.

CHAPTER 4
California Farm Life

Grandmother Sitton lived in Riverbank, and Wilma loved spending time with her. After all, the Mankillers had chosen San Francisco to be closer to her.

When Wilma arrived at the ranch, Grandma welcomed her into her arms. They hugged and went inside to eat something. Grandma listened as Wilma shared her problems. After Wilma finished, Grandma picked up the telephone, dialed Charley and said, "Pearl's here. You better come get her."

Wilma was devastated. But it was the right thing to do. Wilma was young and she belonged with her family.

Charley arrived later that day and drove her back to Daly City.

Wilma didn't give up. She saved her money and ran away again. Grandma Sitton comforted her and called her father again. Charley drove out and picked her up. Wilma ran away again a third time, then a fourth time. After the fifth time, her parents understood she wouldn't stop running away from San Francisco.

Grandma Sitton eventually sold her ranch and moved to Escalon, where her son owned a dairy farm. Wilma's parents gave permission for her to move to the farm for one year. Everyone else agreed. So when she was thirteen, Wilma moved to the dairy farm to live with Grandma Sitton, Uncle Floyd and Aunt Frauline, and their four children—Tommy, Mary Louise, Teddie, and Eddie, who were twins about Wilma's age.

When she first arrived on the dairy farm, Wilma had conflicts with her cousins. She hoped to start fresh and make new friends. But her cousins had warned their classmates that even Wilma's parents couldn't control her, that she had a bad attitude, and that they should keep their distance. Wilma ate lunch by herself and had no one to sit with at recess.

The rivalry between Wilma and her four cousins continued because they all had competitive personalities. Wilma described their relationship as "pure country," meaning none of them would run from a fight. She had learned to protect herself and would not soften. Her moody attitude kept others away.

One hot afternoon, while they walked back from working in the fields with Uncle Floyd, Teddie pulled Wilma's hair one time too many. She had had enough of his teasing and walloped him. Her surprise punch knocked him down. Of course, her actions had consequences that included a threat to send her back to the city. Wilma settled down. So did her cousins, and the teasing stopped.

Wilma noticed that once she stood up for herself and changed her attitude, her life on the farm improved. Wilma felt better. Her daily routine started at 5:00 a.m., when she milked the cows with her cousins. Next, she removed the soiled straw in the animal stalls and replaced it with fresh straw.

Her job was to keep the barn clean. She relaxed after school by exploring the fields and swimming in nearby creeks.

Wilma spent a lot of time with Grandma Sitton. She was one of the hardest-working people Wilma knew besides her dad. Grandma loved gardening. She and Wilma talked about many topics while they picked peaches.

While harvesting fruit, Grandma spoke freely, sharing her strong opinions. Wilma heard her energetic grandmother sing hymns all day long. Her positive spirit filled Wilma's heart with a can-do attitude and a strong work ethic. Hard work and fresh air were healing.

Wilma believed her grandma shaped her thinking about how to live a good life. Grandma Sitton was strict, but not judgmental, which helped Wilma gain confidence in herself.

After her year in Escalon, her father came to bring Wilma home. But they didn't drive back to Daly City. Her parents had moved to a new town called Hunters Point.

CHAPTER 5
Refuge During Restless Times

Big changes happened while Wilma spent a year living on the farm. Her older brother Don met a Choctaw woman named LeVena at the American Indian Center, married her, and moved away. Taking his salary contribution out of the family budget forced the Mankillers to sell their house in Daly City and find a new one. They found an affordable home in a place called Hunters Point.

Most of the residents there were poor and lived isolated on a peninsula in San Francisco Bay. The largest employer in the area was a shipyard that had closed after World War II, and jobs were scarce. Families struggled.

The Mankiller home was small but comfortable. And clean, unlike some of the other places they had lived, which had rats. Wilma felt safe inside. At the top of the hill, in the distance, the city lights of downtown San Francisco sparkled at night.

San Francisco seen from Hunters Point

Wilma and her sister Linda shared a room on the second floor. They peered out the window at their new community, taking in all the sights and sounds. Wilma played records of jazz and blues greats like Etta James, Sarah Vaughan, and B.B. King while she and her sister danced, talked about boys, and put on makeup with their friends. Cultures clashed on the streets below between African American and Samoan American gangs. In the 1960s, the sisters observed a shift in society where strong women became the heads of households, specifically single mothers. Wilma's experience growing up in Hunters Point

Etta James, B.B. King, and Sarah Vaughan

was unique because of the rare combination of cultures represented there.

Wilma remembered how her neighbors back on the reservation relied on one another for support and survival, "sometimes trading goods—eggs for milk or farm goods for store-bought goods" to get by. She witnessed a similar adaptability in Hunters Point.

Later in life, Wilma reflected on her experiences growing up in this environment. No matter how frustrating their situations became, these women never gave up. Wilma felt connected to them, and observed that "Cherokee identity is tied to . . . a collective determination to follow a good path, be responsible and loving, and help one another . . . to not let go of one another." These women were Wilma's role models because they cared for their community.

But at the time, living with the pressures of

poverty and urban life as a young girl, Wilma was burdened with anxiety and despair. Growing up in Hunters Point was "like one long, hot, boring, lazy afternoon—nothing to do, no place to go, and no promise of anything better in the future."

Eventually, the Mankillers found the San Francisco Indian Center on the edge of the Mission District neighborhood. This new community center became a safe place for Wilma.

American Indian Center, San Francisco

She later remembered: "A moody and self-absorbed teenager could count on one thing—at the end of the day, everything seemed brighter at the Indian Center." She enjoyed reading, listening to music, and talking to other Native people. There were picnics, sports, bingo, and powwows (American Indian gatherings that celebrate cultural traditions and include singing, dancing, eating, and connecting with relatives).

The San Francisco Indian Center provided refuge for its members. A growing sense of pride stirred inside young people, including Wilma. She graduated from high school in June 1963, when she was seventeen, and moved into an apartment with her older sister Frances. She found a job. Wilma developed a sense of independence.

A neighbor introduced her to a soccer player from Ecuador. His full name was Hector Hugo Olaya de Bardi, but Wilma always called him by his middle name, Hugo.

The Civil Rights Movement

After the US Civil War, the practice of segregation in the South (which prohibited Black Americans from using the same school buildings, churches, restaurants, and buses as white people) was put in place to discriminate against Black Americans and other minority groups.

By the 1950s and '60s, people were fighting for equal rights for everyone regardless of skin color, gender, nationality, religion, disability, and age. This was the Civil Rights Movement. Civil rights include the right to vote, the right to a public education, and the right to a fair trial. Activists pushed for protection of these rights by law.

One important civil rights leader, Dr. Martin Luther King Jr., promoted nonviolent protests such as sit-ins and boycotts. His ideas spread across communities and grew. On August 28, 1963, more than two hundred thousand people (both Black and white) marched together in Washington, DC, where Dr. King gave his memorable "I Have a Dream" speech, which rallied civil rights advocates across the country.

Hugo and Wilma fell in love. They married on November 13, 1963. Then in January 1964, Wilma became ill, and her father took her to the hospital. She discovered she had a kidney infection, and that she was pregnant! Hugo and Wilma welcomed a baby girl in August 1964 and named her Felicia.

Hugo went to college during the day and worked at night. Wilma stayed home cooking, cleaning, and taking care of her baby. In June 1966, they had another daughter, who they named Gina.

In the 1960s, Americans watched as protests, rallies, sit-ins, and marches took place in cities across the United States. Many were on college campuses. Most were nonviolent. But violent riots occurred, too. And the nation endured the assassination of a beloved president, John F. Kennedy, in November 1963. They also witnessed newly sworn in President Lyndon B. Johnson send more troops into combat in the Vietnam War.

Wilma changed.

Students protest the Vietnam War on a college campus

The Vietnam War

The Vietnam War began in 1954 and ended in 1975. The costly conflict in Southeast Asia was a civil war between North and South Vietnam. North Vietnam supported communism (a form of government based on creating and sharing wealth that is not based on individual ownership) while South Vietnam fought against it. Australia, South Korea, New Zealand, Thailand, and the Philippines helped the South Vietnamese while the communist governments of the Soviet Union and China joined forces with North Vietnam. The United States joined with South Vietnam because US leaders believed in democracy, not communism, and wanted to help.

In August 1964, President Lyndon B. Johnson expanded the role of the US in the war after the North Vietnamese attacked two US warships.

By 1968, over five hundred thousand US troops were fighting in Vietnam. But many in the US protested the war, which they felt had lasted far too long.

In 1973, both sides agreed to stop fighting. But the war did not end. In 1974, the United States limited military aid to the South Vietnamese. Their army fell apart and couldn't fend off the North Vietnamese, who then invaded. On April 30, 1975, the war ended, and Communist North Vietnam won.

In 1976, North and South Vietnam united into one country, called Vietnam.

College women rally for peace

She watched news reports on TV of the Free Speech Movement, a protest led by college students to remove restrictions on speech. Wilma observed a women's movement begin. "I saw women standing up and speaking out," she recalled. During this time, Wilma wondered about her traditional role as a stay-at-home wife. As her twenty-first birthday approached, doubts crowded her mind. "I would come home . . . and wonder what I was doing, what the future really held for me."

CHAPTER 6
Activist, Leader

In November 1969, a group of Native Americans occupied a San Francisco Bay island. Alcatraz, a maximum-security prison nicknamed "the Rock," was on a desolate island and had closed in 1963. A group of young activists coordinated the takeover of Alcatraz Island.

Alcatraz Island

Eighty-nine Native activists, including men, women, and children, ferried boats across the gray Pacific waters, past a coast guard blockade, and climbed onto the site of the former prison. They reclaimed Alcatraz Island in the name of Indians of all tribes, citing an old treaty that said unused government land could be reverted back to Indian Territory. (A treaty is a formal agreement between two or more nations that goes into effect when all parties agree to the responsibilities laid out in the document. Treaties are binding, which means there are legal consequences for breaking one.) The activists declared the right to take the land back using the government's own words in a legal document.

For over a year and a half, boatloads of people arrived to occupy the old prison site. The population grew to one thousand people on Alcatraz at times. Daily life was organized by an elected council who set up school for the children, organized meals, and established a health-care clinic.

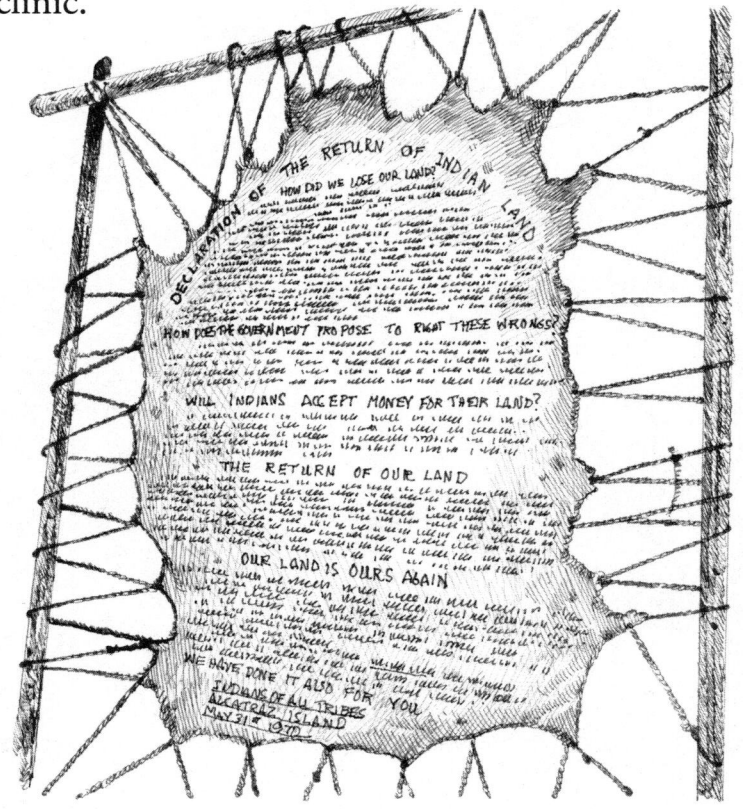

Tribal members from many nations populated the island. People came from Alaska, Oklahoma, South Dakota, Montana, and other places.

Musicians and celebrities showed up to support their cause. Newspapers and TV reporters interviewed tribal leaders on Alcatraz. All in all, it was a peaceful occupation.

Wilma's brother Richard was the first of her siblings to hop on a boat. Wilma, Linda, and

several of her other siblings followed his lead and
went out for a visit. Staying on the island wasn't an
option for Wilma. Her children and her husband
were at home. Wilma figured out another way
to support the takeover. She collected food and
clothing to distribute to those on the island.

She helped spread the word, handing out flyers.
Wilma took her daughters for a tour of Alcatraz
during the occupation, too.

Hugo opposed her activism. He wanted her
to be a more traditional wife and stay-at-home
mother.

Wilma said, "Although I knew something was
terribly wrong with my marriage, I tried to stick
it out."

In addition to volunteering, Wilma often visited her parents. They were finally enjoying a simple life in their small home in a new town. After dinner one night, Charley told Wilma how proud he was of her.

Wilma noticed her father growing more ill. Then she heard the devastating news. He was diagnosed with a disease that caused kidney infections and kidney failure. Wilma went to Alcatraz Island and told her siblings to come home. Charley died on February 20, 1971, at age fifty-six, in the company of his family. The family brought his body back to Oklahoma to bury him in the family cemetery. Cherokee people, some from as far as Kansas and North Carolina,

attended the services for Charley Mankiller. Wilma went back to California after the funeral. She found comfort in her work with the Native community.

After nineteen months of the Alcatraz occupation, the last of the occupants were ushered off the island by federal marshals in June 1971. Alcatraz not only awakened a sleepy United States about Native American issues but also stirred something inside Wilma.

She knew she had a difficult decision to make about her life.

People leave Alcatraz Island

Wilma relied on skills she developed when she volunteered at the Indian Center in San Francisco and accepted the role of director of the Native American Youth Center in Oakland. She recruited volunteers. She organized school curricula and inspired students. Everyone was welcome.

While working on a renovation project, she needed money and manpower. Wilma knew the owner of a local business called Chicken's Place, a spot where Native people spent time. She walked inside and asked for volunteers. Many people jumped up from their seats to offer support in any way they could. They were ready to help. Wilma was surprised.

After that, Wilma visited Chicken's Place whenever she needed help. She said, "I formed a belief that poor people, particularly poor American Indian people, have a lot more potential and many more answers to problems than they are ever given a chance to realize."

Wilma also realized that in order to help other Native people, she'd need a car. Hugo didn't agree, so Wilma bought her own car. She traveled to help other tribal communities in California. She had changed from a traditional housewife to a self-reliant, active leader. Hugo and Wilma spent less and less time together.

Wilma said, "Whenever I do pause to reflect, I find that many of my hopes and aspirations [dreams] were formed during those wonderfully sad and crazy years of the 1960s in San Francisco."

CHAPTER 7
Pit River

In the early 1970s, Wilma volunteered to help the Pit River Tribe of Northern California in their fight against Pacific Gas and Electric (PG&E). The Pit River people wanted their ancestral lands back, which in 1959, the US government had admitted to stealing. About one hundred people occupied a PG&E campsite. Police officers and Forest Service agents arrested some of them and forced them off the site. Wilma worked in the Pit River offices, organizing papers for their legal defense. She gained valuable knowledge about treaty rights and international law while she worked for the Pit River Tribe. But the Pit River Tribe was not successful in getting their land back.

During the nearly five years Wilma worked with the Pit River Tribe, she and her daughters spent time with Pit River elders. They stayed with Raymond and Marie Lego in a small cabin on their land, which included a garden and wooded areas nearby. They lived a simple, happy life. Wilma later wrote, "I felt at home there. . . . The demeanor and lifestyle of the Pit River people put me in mind of my own people back in eastern Oklahoma."

The Lego home became a meeting place for others. Wilma recalled, "In the evening, we sat on the front porch, and Raymond and Marie told us about their long struggle to get back the land. Sometimes Raymond would bring out an old cardboard box filled with tribal letters and documents, which he treated as though they were sacred objects. We were privileged to be able to see those things and to spend that time with such people."

Wilma, Felicia, and Gina visited other places,

like Mendocino, home of the Pomo people. They harvested seaweed and carried it in heirloom baskets—those that had belonged to their families for generations. Wilma remembered, "The seaweed was quickly fried in very hot grease and wrapped in thick bread. It was delicious."

She gained knowledge of how others connected to their land, their traditions, and their ceremonies.

During this time, Wilma and Hugo grew further apart.

"All of those trips and visits. All of the music and dancing. All of the hard, hard work. All of the time spent in the fight for Alcatraz, at the youth center, with the Pit River people gave me precious knowledge. All of the people I encountered—the militants, the wise elders, the keepers of the medicine, the storytellers—were my teachers, my best teachers. I knew my education would never be complete. In a way, it was only beginning. I felt like a newborn whose eyes have just opened to the first light."

Wilma's focus shifted, turning away from the California coastline. She envisioned her life in the East, a place of new beginnings. Her memories of when she was a ten-year-old girl being forced to leave her homeland shone brightly in her mind. The trees, the sounds of the birds, her relatives, Mankiller Flats, all the

things she took notice of when they left were calling her home to Oklahoma. She decided to divorce Hugo and move back to Mankiller Flats.

In 1977, after twenty-one years of living in California, Wilma moved back to Oklahoma with her daughters, Gina and Felicia, now eleven and thirteen.

CHAPTER 8
The Bell Water Project

Wilma and the girls moved in with her mother, who had just moved back to Oklahoma herself. She tried to find a job, but it was a challenge. She had been gone for over twenty years. Some people now considered her an outsider.

She didn't give up hope and kept busy sewing ribbon shirts for her family. (Indigenous women proudly wear skirts decorated with silky ribbons. Similarly, ribbon shirts worn by men are a symbol of Native identity.)

Wilma enjoyed sewing, playing the guitar, and later in life, writing poetry.

In October 1977, she landed a job and became the new economic stimulus coordinator for the Cherokee Nation of Oklahoma. Wilma's job was to provide guidance about new business and redevelopment projects for the tribal office. Wilma had experience in writing grant proposals (requests for money given for a specific purpose) to help raise outside money for tribal projects. For the next two years her work increased the income of the tribe.

Wilma also decided to finish her college degree. She drove about an hour each way to her college campus. On the morning of November 9, 1979, Wilma took the day off from classes to visit the Cherokee Nation personnel director in Tahlequah. On her way, she was involved in a serious car crash. Wilma survived, but she had to endure more than a year in recovery from the accident and other health issues. Finally, she went back to work.

In 1981, she earned a new job title, director of the Cherokee Nation Community Development Department. Wilma's first assignment was to lead a project in one of the poorest communities in Cherokee Nation—Bell, Oklahoma. She met Charlie Soap, a full-blooded bilingual Cherokee and her partner on the project. Since many of those living in Bell spoke only Cherokee, Charlie bridged the communication gap by speaking both Cherokee and English.

Charlie Soap

Many residents of Bell didn't have access to indoor plumbing. They walked to their nearby school building to get clean water from the only spigot in town. Community access to clean water—a basic right for human beings—was about to slip away. So Wilma and Charlie set up a town meeting to find out what they needed. Wilma believed people should try to solve their own problems. When they arrived, no one in the community showed up. They didn't trust outsiders.

They set up another date, and then another. The third time, twelve people showed up and discussed the question, "What single thing would change this community the most"?

Charlie and Wilma also went door to door to ask people what they needed. They wanted access to clean water in their homes so their kids could bathe and eat meals before school.

Wilma called another meeting to explain that if grant money was given by the government, it would supply equipment and materials, but each of the 103 Bell families would need to complete 350 hours of digging trenches, hauling stones, and connecting sixteen miles of pipe. Those who worked would get fresh water inside their homes.

For months Charlie worked side by side with Wilma, digging and filling trenches, too.

Unfortunately, the grant money excluded white people in Bell and only supported Cherokee Nation citizens. The community revived a spirit of *gadugi*, meaning "to work together for the good of the community and future generations." Wilma explained, "Even if families didn't like each other, they were learning to work together."

Native neighbors had bake sales and other fundraisers for their white neighbors. They raised enough money so every family in Bell could have clean water.

After more than a year, the residents of Bell completed the water project. Homes now had access to clean water.

The Bell Water Project was a success. Students' grades increased. Dropout rates fell. Then the community members set their sights on the next problem—repairing existing homes. They built twenty-one new structures and a community center for everyone to enjoy.

News reporters heard about the project and brought cameras to report on the people of Bell.

As Bell residents saw themselves on TV, they developed pride in themselves and their community. The Bell project showed the nation that if people worked together, impossible things could be done.

The Bell project inspired others and sparked a movement across other Cherokee communities like Burnt Cabin, Wild Horse, and Briggs.

While Wilma worked, her girls studied and did well in school. They made new friends, and so did Wilma. Charlie became her best friend, and their relationship grew. They fell in love and got married.

Wilma's experience with the Bell project deepened her desire to help others, which led her to politics.

In 1983, Principal Chief Swimmer was up for reelection and wanted a deputy chief who would work alongside Cherokee people to meet their needs. In Chief Swimmer's mind, Wilma already showed what he was looking for in a running mate. He asked Wilma to run for office as his deputy principal chief in Cherokee Nation's next election.

Wilma was an activist, not a politician, and declined. After their conversation, she went out to a rural area in Oklahoma for another project. She met a family of three who lived in an abandoned bus with no roof. This was not the only family Wilma observed living this way. Wilma wanted to help and realized how she could.

She drove back to Chief Swimmer and told him she had changed her mind. She said yes to his proposal and became his running mate. Little did she know she would face major obstacles in the near future.

CHAPTER 9
Leading Her Cherokee People

Running a successful campaign means candidates must meet and interact with many people in the community. Wilma met people who opposed her not for her beliefs but for her gender. Some of the men thought that Cherokees would be laughed at if they elected a woman as deputy chief. The more Wilma heard things like this, the more she knew she had made the right decision.

Some opponents used scare tactics. Wilma received hate mail and death threats, and had her tires slashed after a meeting. Once, she answered the phone and heard a rifle being loaded. During a parade, a man pretended to fire a gun at her. She turned her head away. The scare tactics didn't work. Wilma knew she was doing the right thing.

She relied on her experience as a community organizer in San Francisco and knew how to bring people together.

After the ballots were counted on election day, Wilma discovered she beat opponent J. B. Dreadfulwater, but had to face off the other woman running for deputy chief. Her name was Agnes Cowan. In July, Wilma beat Cowan and won the election. Wilma became the first female deputy chief in Cherokee history. She was sworn into office on August 14, 1983.

As deputy chief, Wilma became president of the tribal council. Her job was a challenge because some council members did not support her. Wilma stayed on course. She committed to revitalizing and rebuilding communities in the fourteen counties in Cherokee Nation.

Then in September 1985, Chief Swimmer announced he was leaving. President Ronald Reagan had offered Swimmer a job. Swimmer's

new post was quite an honor—head of the Bureau of Indian Affairs in Washington, DC. His resignation allowed his deputy chief to fill the open spot.

Wilma became the first woman principal chief of the Cherokee Nation. On December 5, 1985, she put her hand on the bible and recited her oath:

"I, Wilma P. Mankiller, do solemnly swear, or affirm, that I will faithfully execute the duties of Principal Chief of the Cherokee Nation. And will, to the best of my abilities, preserve, protect, and defend the Constitutions of the Cherokee Nation and the United States of America. I swear, or affirm, further that I will do everything within my power to promote culture, heritage, and tradition of the Cherokee Nation."

Cameras clicked and applause welcomed her as she stepped up to the podium. Wilma thanked her community, friends, and family.

The Bureau of Indian Affairs

The Bureau of Indian Affairs (BIA) was established in 1824. At first, the BIA followed federal policies that were designed to trick American Indians and Alaska Natives into accepting American society and culture as their own and assimilating to it.

But much has changed over the past 185 years. Now this bureau in the Department of the Interior of the United States works to maintain relationships between 574 federally recognized tribal nations and the US government.

The BIA's mission statement reads: "Our mission is to enhance the quality of life, promote economic opportunities, and to carry out the federal responsibility entrusted to us to protect and improve the trust assets of American Indians and Alaska Natives."

In 1987, Wilma announced she would run for a second term as principal chief. Her "positive, forward-thinking campaign" was celebrated when she won the election. It was a difficult campaign, not only because she ran against three opponents but also because she became ill.

Her family always supported her work. Wilma's daughter Felicia had married and had a son. Wilma became a grandmother. Their family was growing. But behind the scenes, something else was looming. Wilma's long-term kidney disease wore her down. And Charlie, Felicia, and Gina were growing more worried about her health.

By 1989, they all realized Wilma's kidneys were failing and she needed a transplant. Her family and friends rallied around her through her hospitalizations and her transplant surgery. She said, "Since the operation, I have continued to work as hard as possible for my tribe. . . . There is still much to be done."

Once she recovered, Wilma ran for a third term on her own merits and won in a landslide, proof of her strength and intelligence. This time, her husband Charlie held the bible as she recited her oath on August 14, 1991.

During her three terms, the Cherokee Nation grew. Tribal enrollment increased from 68,000 to 170,000 members. People had access to improved housing and health care. The Institute for Cherokee Literacy, which she created, worked to preserve traditional language and culture. By boosting her people, she fostered a strong sense of Cherokee identity.

Wilma served as principal chief of the Cherokee Nation from 1985 to 1995.

She felt honored to be the first female principal chief but wanted to be remembered as serving others and fostering self-reliance. She increased jobs and improved housing, health care, and education. When she was reelected in 1991 with 82.7 percent of the votes, she united members and won the hearts of the Cherokee Nation. And she did all this while battling her own health problems.

During her terms as principal chief, Wilma didn't let her poor health slow her down. She never complained. She accepted the challenge of a leadership role and made a commitment to serve her people. Her work made her feel complete.

After seventeen years of service, fifty-year-old Wilma retired from politics.

Then, in 1996, she accepted a new role. As a visiting professor at Dartmouth College, she taught Native American law, tribal sovereignty, and women's studies to the next generation. She said, "We need a country full of young, educated Native American people." She traveled around the country to instill pride

in Native people with her words. She wrote

her autobiography, titled *Mankiller: A Chief and Her People*, and essays in a book titled *Every Day Is a Good Day*.

Soon she became ill again, this time with cancer. She underwent chemotherapy treatments in Boston. Although the treatments fought her cancer, they also damaged her kidneys.

Wilma endured another kidney transplant.

Back on her feet, she spoke to groups all over about Native sovereignty and women's issues. In 2005, she taught a class at the University of Oregon and spoke about tribal history and culture.

Wilma received many awards in her lifetime, including the Presidential Medal of Freedom, which was presented to her in 1998 by then-president Bill Clinton.

The Presidential Medal of Freedom

The Presidential Medal of Freedom was established in 1963 by US president John F. Kennedy. It is the country's highest civilian award. The award is presented by the president, who chooses the honorees, to recognize positive contributions to the country, to other cultures, or in promoting world peace.

Past recipients include astronaut Neil Armstrong (1969), First Lady of the United States Lady Bird Johnson (1977), Dr. Martin Luther King Jr. (1977), marine biologist Rachel Carson (1980), actor and Brigadier General James Stewart (1985), Prime Minister of the United Kingdom Margaret Thatcher (1991), blues singer-songwriter B.B. King (2006), and many more.

When her doctors diagnosed her pancreatic cancer in 2010, Wilma issued a statement in a newspaper. She said, "I can't control the challenges the Creator sends my way, but I can control the way I think about them and deal with them. On balance, I have been blessed with an extraordinarily rich and wonderful life."

On April 6, 2010, Wilma Pearl Mankiller walked on, which is a traditional way for Native people to say she died. She was a role model for her family, for tribal leaders, and for young women who can now dream of becoming tribal leaders. She encouraged them when she said, "If you want to see a leader, look in the mirror."

A quote etched on her gravestone reads, "I want to be remembered as the person who helped us restore faith in ourselves."

The Wilma Mankiller Foundation was created in 2010. Its goal is to support community projects and provide educational opportunities for Native people. In 2013, *The Cherokee Word for Water*, a movie about Wilma's work in the Bell Water Project, was released with support from the foundation.

In 2022, the US Mint honored Wilma by releasing a Wilma Mankiller coin as part of the American Women Quarters Program.

In November 2023, Mattel released a Wilma Mankiller Barbie. She wears a teal green dress decorated with ribbons on the skirt. The doll comes with a miniature heirloom basket. Principal Chief Chuck Hoskin Jr. celebrated the honor with this statement:

"When Native girls see it, they can achieve it, and Wilma Mankiller has shown countless young women to be fearless and speak up for Indigenous and Human rights. She not only served in a role dominated by men during a time that tribal nations were suppressed, but she led. Wilma Mankiller is a champion for the Cherokee Nation, for Indian Country and even my own daughter. She truly exemplifies leadership, culture and equality and we applaud Mattel for commemorating her in the Barbie Inspiring Women Series."

Wilma Mankiller
Barbie

Principal Chief Wilma P. Mankiller supported basic human rights for her people. She improved lives. Wilma's legacy and her connection to her Cherokee community will not be forgotten.

Timeline of Wilma Mankiller's Life

1945 — Wilma Pearl Mankiller is born on November 18 in Tahlequah, Oklahoma

1956 — Relocates to San Francisco, California

1963 — Graduates high school in June

— Marries Hector Hugo Olaya de Bardi in November

1969 — Joins the Alcatraz Island occupation

1974 — Divorces Hugo

1977 — Moves back to Oklahoma with her daughters

— Begins working for the Cherokee Nation

1981 — Becomes director of the Bell Water Project

1983 — Elected deputy principal chief of the Cherokee Nation

1985 — Becomes first female principal chief of the Cherokee Nation

1986 — Marries Charlie Soap in October

1993 — Publishes *Mankiller: A Chief and Her People*

1995 — Retires as principal chief of the Cherokee Nation

1998 — Receives the Presidential Medal of Freedom in a White House ceremony

2010 — Dies of pancreatic cancer on April 6 at age sixty-four

— Wilma Mankiller Foundation established

2023 — Mattel releases the Wilma Mankiller Barbie doll

Timeline of the World

1945	World War II ends
1968	American Indian Movement (AIM) is established in Minnesota to improve living conditions for Native Americans who had relocated to cities
1969	The Apollo 11 lunar lander, *Eagle*, lands on the moon
1970	First Earth Day is celebrated to raise awareness of environmental issues
1972	Congress passes the Clean Water Act, which made a commitment to protecting the nation's water
1980	First Rubik's Cube sold
1990	South African activist Nelson Mandela is released after twenty-seven years in prison
1993	Michael Jordan retires from the NBA to play baseball, then returns to the NBA nearly a year and a half later
1994	Nelson Mandela is elected the first Black president of South Africa
2005	YouTube officially launches in December
2010	A volcano in southern Iceland erupts on April 14, spewing enormous clouds of ash into the air and disrupting air traffic across Europe
2020	Shutdowns begin in response to the global COVID-19 pandemic

Bibliography

*Books for young readers

Bliss, Tamrala Swafford. *Wilma Mankiller: A Life in American History*. Santa Barbara, CA: ABC-CLIO, 2023.

Brando, Elizabeth. "Wilma Mankiller (1945–2010)." *National Women's History Museum*. https://www.womenshistory.org/education-resources/biographies/wilma-mankiller.

*Buckley, Patricia Morris. *The First Woman Cherokee Chief: Wilma Pearl Mankiller*. New York: Random House Children's Books, 2023.

Herda, D. J. *Wilma Mankiller: How One Woman United the Cherokee Nation and Helped Change the Face of America*. Guilford, CT: TwoDot, 2021.

Mankiller, Wilma. *Every Day Is a Good Day*. Golden, CO: Fulcrum Publishing, 2004.

Mankiller, Wilma. "Wilma Mankiller: Principal Chief, Cherokee Nation." Interview by John Erling. *Voices of Oklahoma*, August 13, 2009. https://voicesofoklahoma.com/interviews/mankiller-wilma/.

Mankiller, Wilma, and Michael Wallis. ***Mankiller: A Chief and Her People***. New York: St. Martin's Press, 1993.

National Archives. "American Indian Urban Relocation." US National Archives and Records Administration. Updated March 3, 2023. https://www.archives.gov/education/lessons/ indian-relocation.html.

*Sorell, Traci. ***She Persisted: Wilma Mankiller***. New York: Philomel, 2022.

"Wilma Mankiller: Governance, Leadership and the Cherokee Nation." Produced by Native Nations Institute. University of Arizona, September 29, 2008. Video, 44:59. https:// nnigovernance.arizona.edu/wilma-mankiller-governance- leadership-and-cherokee-nation.